QUIET THE VOICE AMPLIFY THE RESULTS

How to Overcome Self Doubt and Lead with Confidence

ORLA KELLY
PUBLISHING

Michelle DeStefano

978-1-917728-20-1

To my father, Michael X. DeStefano, an English teacher, a writer, and a truth-teller who saw the world for what it was, and loved it anyway.

You left a lasting legacy with your students, but to me,
you were a guide through the highs and lows of life.

You taught me that how we respond to life's challenges shapes who we become, for ourselves and for others. You showed me the power of following my True North, living with humility and kindness, and never forgetting to smile and laugh along the way.

Here's to you, Dad—in heaven, and always in my heart.

Michelle

Contents

Who This Book Is for and Why It Matters

Imagine walking into a boardroom or meeting where you're expected to lead with authority. On the outside, you look polished and prepared, but inside, a voice whispers: *Are you really qualified to be here?* You're not alone, and you're not the only one feeling that way.

This book is for high-achieving professionals like you: leaders who are navigating intense challenges, relentless pressure, and even moments of self-doubt while striving to perform at their best. If you've ever felt like your external image of success doesn't always match your internal dialogue, this is the guide you've been waiting for.

More specifically, it's written for healthcare leaders, senior executives, emerging change makers, and corporate professionals who are ready to tackle challenges such as:

• How to thrive in high-stakes, high-pressure environments
• How to deal with being undervalued or overlooked
• How to silence self-doubt that stops you from reaching your full potential

If you've been a dependable team player while quietly battling your insecurities, this book is designed to help you pivot.

Through powerful stories, actionable frameworks, and introspective exercises, you'll learn how to:

• Quiet that inner critic and rewrite its fear-driven narrative into one of empowerment
• Identify patterns that hold you back, so you can take charge with confidence

- Transform limiting beliefs into bold, goal-driven actions that position you for greater success

This isn't theory. This is about stepping into the authentic leader you were always destined to be.

The doubts that have held you back? **You can replace them.**

The voice that questions your authority? **You can quiet and reframe it.**

It's your time to lead with purpose, clarity, and conviction.

The only question is:

Are you ready to take the first step?

Open the first page and start becoming the bold, confident leader you're meant to be.

About the Author

Michelle DeStefano is the CEO/Founder of Michelle DeStefano Executive Coaching, and a nationally recognized executive coach with a mission: to help high-performing professionals overcome self-doubt, amplify their leadership presence, and step into the rooms they belong in—without waiting for permission.

With over four decades of leadership experience, including serving as a Chief Nursing Officer, Michelle understands firsthand the pressure, politics, and performance demands that shape (and sometimes silence) today's healthcare leaders. Her coaching practice is rooted in both lived experience and advanced professional training, blending behavioral tools like CliftonStrengths and DISC with deep insight into organizational dynamics. Michelle is an accredited coach via the European Mentoring and Coaching Council, a certified John Maxwell Team Leader, and a John Maxwell Advanced Behavioral Analysis Consultant.

Michelle has worked with senior executives, physician leaders, directors, and emerging changemakers across the country. Whether coaching a nurse leader through a career pivot or helping a VP navigate a high-stakes transition, her work centers around one belief: **you don't have to wait to be perfect to be powerful.**

Her personal story runs parallel to the leaders she serves. As an identical twin, Michelle learned early how identity, comparison, and internal narratives can shape the way we lead, speak up, and see ourselves. That experience seeded a lifelong passion for helping others quiet the inner critic and reconnect with their most authentic leadership voice.

Through Executive Coaching programs, workshops, speaking engagements, and now this book, Michelle continues to help leaders *like you* silence the noise, reclaim their clarity, and lead from a place of alignment, confidence, and influence.

Career Progression

Chief Nursing Officer - July 2012-2016

Senior Solutions Consultant - September 2017-February 2019

JMT Certified Coach, Speaker, Trainer 2019

Independent Business Development Consultant - April 2019-August 2022

CEO/Founder of Michelle DeStefano Executive Coaching - October 2021-current

Conscious Coaching Academy Candidate and Graduate - May 2024

I'm Not Lisa… My Name is Michelle

(A nod to the song—and a truth I've lived my whole life.)

There's an old country song that stopped me in my tracks the first time I heard it.It begins, *"I'm not Lisa… my name is Julie."* It's a quiet lament—a woman caught in someone else's story, constantly mistaken, unseen for who she truly is.

And I felt that in my bones. Because for most of my life, I've been called by the wrong name, labeled with someone else's traits, or slotted into a role I didn't choose. Not because people were cruel, but because I was born an identical twin.

I'm Michelle. The older twin by six minutes. And those six minutes meant something. I wore them like a badge of honor. They made me the firstborn. The responsible one. My father's namesake.

And with that came an unspoken assignment: *Support your sister.* So I did. I outlined the chapters of our textbooks. I handed her my notes to study from. I learned early that 'helpful' meant 'valuable.' And I took that role seriously.

But over time, what started as family loyalty quietly turned into something heavier: **comparison.**

"She's the bubbly one, right?"
"You're the grounded one."
"Oh, you must be the serious one."

What began as playful labels became limiting definitions. And somewhere in that split, I stopped seeing myself clearly.

But here's the part that still gives me pause: Despite looking exactly alike, my twin and I could always tell our identical baby dolls apart. Can you imagine that? Two Chatty Cathy dolls, side by side, and we just *knew* whose was whose. Mine had slightly brighter eyes. Slightly rosier cheeks. My parents were amazed. They called it a sign of intelligence, of connection.

But in truth? It was something deeper. It was vigilance. It was constant comparison. It was the beginning of a lifelong habit of scanning for small differences, for signs of identity, for a way to feel separate... and seen.

That habit stayed with me.
It shaped me.
It became my inner critic.

Not a loud, angry voice, but a quiet one. A whisper that told me to stay in the background. To work hard, honor authority, and speak only when I had something flawless to say.

And I listened. I became accomplished. Composed. Strategic. But inside? I felt like a diminished version of myself. Like I had to dim my light to keep the peace. To not be "too much." To not take up space that hadn't been pre-approved.

Maybe your story is different. Maybe you weren't a twin. But maybe— just maybe—you were given a role that didn't quite fit. Maybe you've been assigned traits, responsibilities, or expectations that no longer match who you really are.

If you've ever questioned your seat at the table...
If you've ever doubted your voice, even when others praised your competence...
If you've ever felt like you were playing small, even while performing big...
Then you know the voice I'm talking about.

This book is about that voice. The inner critic that grew up beside you and now follows you into every boardroom, every decision, every sleepless night. But more than that, this book is about the voice beneath that voice. The one that's been waiting patiently. The one that remembers your values, your brilliance, your purpose.

It's time to stop mistaking yourself for someone you're not.
It's time to reclaim your name.
Your story.
Your power.

Let's begin.

CHAPTER 1

CHAPTER 1

Understanding the Inner Critic

The inner critic is loud, but it's not the voice of truth. Don't let it run the show.

Long before we ever name her, the inner critic has already taken up space in our minds. She whispers doubts before we step into meetings. She questions our competence, even when we check every box. She is shaped by our past but impacts our present in ways we rarely acknowledge.

So What Exactly *Is* the Inner Critic?

The inner critic is that internal voice of self-doubt and judgment that questions your worth, your capability, or your right to belong, especially when you're stepping into something new, bold, or unfamiliar. She is shaped by early experiences, authority figures, cultural messages, and even moments you've long forgotten. Sometimes, she's loud and brash. Other times, she's quiet and polished. But she always holds you back from your full expression.

Until we understand where our inner critic came from and how she works, we unconsciously let her lead.

Where Does This Voice Come From?

The inner critic is shaped by the stories we've lived, the subtle patterns and quiet messages that taught us how to survive, succeed, or stay small. Drawing from my own experiences and the courageous leaders I coach, here are some of the most common origins:

- Invisible Expectations in Childhood
- Authority-Induced Self-Doubt
- Perfectionism Disguised as Professionalism
- Critique That Becomes a Cage
- Comparison and Social Media Pressure
- Rewarded Self-Silencing
- Polish Over Presence
- Fear of Not Measuring Up to Metrics
- Performing Instead of Belonging

These aren't abstract ideas; they're lived experiences. The stories that follow reveal how these patterns take root and play out in real life. Whether it's childhood roles, institutional critique, or the weight of professional polish, each one reflects a deeper message that shaped our inner voice. As you read, you might recognize parts of your own story, and begin to see that the inner critic isn't just personal. She's patterned, practiced, and often inherited.

Early Childhood and the Creation of Strong Limiting Beliefs

For me, she appeared in childhood, long before I even knew what self-talk was. As I shared in the Introduction, being the 'responsible twin' came with invisible expectations. Her voice only grew louder as I navigated school and eventually entered nursing. Steadfast and quiet, I yearned for a bigger personality, but those early experiences had already stifled it.

Perfection Disguised as Professionalism

I'll never forget the moment in nursing school when a faculty member looked at me and asked:

"Do you really know what's going on with your patients, or do you just look like you do?"

That question stopped me cold.

I wasn't just being evaluated—I was being questioned at the level of identity. Suddenly, the way I carried myself—professional, polished, pulled together—wasn't seen as strength. It was seen as a mask. From that day on, a seed of doubt took root: **Is my competence real? Or just cosmetic?** I hadn't yet named my inner critic, but she had already found her way in.

The World of "Perfect" We Scroll Through

The inner critic doesn't just live in our memories.
She thrives in our culture.

Take a scroll through social media. What do you see? Perfectly curated meals. Flawless family portraits. Picture-perfect vacations. It's as if everyone's life is being narrated by a lifestyle guru.

One of my clients—let's call her Amanda—shared how she used to think her greatest achievement would be being the "perfect wife and mother." That's what she was praised for. They're the roles she performed. But deep inside, as a scientist with a doctoral degree, she knew she was capable of more. And the more she compared her life to others online, the more she felt the disconnect between who she was and who she was pretending to be. She had what it took to be more, but she played small, because that's what her inner programming told her to do. Social media doesn't create the inner critic, but it certainly gives her a megaphone.

When Critique Becomes a Cage

Let me introduce you to Gloria. Highly accomplished. Holding a doctorate degree. Deeply respected by her peers. And yet, the thought of speaking up in boardrooms made her freeze.

Why?

Because early in her career, when she dared to speak up in high-level meetings, she wasn't guided—she was criticized. Abruptly. Publicly. Harshly. Not for her ideas, but for her delivery. Her tone. Her confidence.

Now, years later, Gloria still second-guesses herself in rooms where she undeniably belongs. She has the credentials, the experience, and the leadership capability.

Yet, she struggles to accept this and continues to hold back from pursuing the role of Chief Nursing Officer, a position she would love and is fully qualified for.

Why? Because the inner critic whispers:

"You don't know how to speak in meetings."
"You're not ready."
"You're not good enough."

The inner critic doesn't care how smart or successful you are. She will find a way to make you question all of it.

Fear of Not Measuring Up

Consider Jane, another client. Jane came to me to build an executive presence and lead more confidently. She was already a doctoral candidate, a nursing policy advocate, and a respected voice in her field. She appeared polished, articulate, and accomplished.

But in our sessions, a deeper truth emerged. Beneath the surface was **a paralyzing fear that if she failed to meet every metric or goal, she would be fired**. It didn't matter how experienced she was or how many accolades she'd earned. If she couldn't hit the target perfectly, she believed she'd lose everything.

When we paused to explore the root cause of this belief, Jane told me a story about her time as a collegiate athlete. After an injury, she fought hard to recover and rejoin her team. But even after regaining her strength, she didn't contribute to a winning season, and she was benched. That early experience left a painful, lasting imprint:

"If I'm not performing at the top, I don't belong."

That same self-imposed pressure followed her into her career, where she led with caution, rather than confidence—always fearing the bench was just around the corner.

Cultural Norms Around Fitting In

Many organizations talk about transparency and inclusion. But when someone speaks up or challenges the status quo, they're suddenly viewed as disruptive or not a team player.

This tension creates a powerful inner critic script:

"If I say what I really think, I'll be seen as difficult."
"Better to blend in than be bold."

This is especially true for women, people of color, and anyone from outside the "default mold" who leads.

When authenticity is punished or misunderstood, the inner critic learns to silence you to protect you. But the cost is high: your voice, your creativity, and your leadership.

Reflection: Meeting Your Inner Critic

Let's pause.

This chapter isn't just about me or Amanda or Jane or Gloria.

It's about *you*.
Your story.
Your moments of doubt.
Your version of the voice.

Take a few minutes to reflect:

- **What early experiences shaped how you see yourself today?**
  Think back to moments when you were praised, misunderstood, or made to feel small.
- **Whose voices shaped your self-perception?**
  Are there people—parents, teachers, supervisors, whose messages still echo in your mind?
- **When do you notice your inner critic showing up most often?**
  In new situations? When you're about to speak up? When you're trying something bold?
- **What does she sound like? What does she say?**
  If you were to write down the most common messages she gives you, what would they be?
- **What part of your story has she tried to keep quiet?**
  What's the truth about you that's been buried beneath the pressure to perform or please?

In the next chapter, we'll find out how to name your inner critic, recognize her patterns, and understand her impact on your life, empowering you to gently loosen her grip. Because awareness is where healing begins.And once we see her clearly, we can finally stop mistaking her for the truth.

CHAPTER 2

CHAPTER 2

The Cost of the Inner Critic

Why Staying Small Costs More than You Think

The inner critic doesn't just speak—it shapes.
It shapes how we lead.
How we respond to pressure.
How we interpret feedback.
How we respond in social settings.
And how we either rise into our influence—or shrink back from it.

The cost of letting the inner critic dominate isn't always obvious. It doesn't always look like failure. Sometimes it looks like overworking. Over-giving. Over-preparing. But inside, it's emotional exhaustion. Missed opportunities. Damaged confidence. And a growing disconnect from the leader, and person, you're meant to be.

Introducing the Saboteurs: The Faces of the Inner Critic

So what are saboteurs exactly?

Saboteurs are the inner critic's many disguises. They're the patterns of self-sabotage we've learned to survive, especially under pressure. They're not random. They're rehearsed. Repeated. Refined. And almost always rooted in fear. These voices may have started as protectors. But now? They limit your growth, your confidence, and your impact.

Shirzad Chamine, author of Positive Influence, had identified nine common saboteurs that I have seen in high performing professionals and healthcare leaders:

- **The Judge:** The loudest voice. Constantly finds what's wrong with you, with others, with situations.
- **The Hyper-Achiever:** Your worth is based on performance. Nothing is ever "enough."
- **The Pleaser:** You seek approval by putting others first, even at your own expense.
- **The Stickler:** Perfectionism in disguise. Everything has to be just right or it's worthless.
- **The Avoider:** Conflict is dangerous. Stay quiet. Don't rock the boat.
- **The Controller:** You feel safest when you're in charge. Delegation feels like weakness.
- **The Victim:** You personalize setbacks and stay trapped in emotional overwhelm.
- **The Restless:** Constant busyness. Jumping to the next thing without grounding in the present.
- **The Hyper-Vigilant:** Always bracing for disaster. The tension never eases.

Amanda: Performing for Praise

Amanda, a highly qualified scientist with a doctorate, spent years trying to 'do it all.' She played the roles of perfect wife, perfect mom, and professional who had all the answers. But deep down, she felt disconnected from it all.

Her inner critic told her she had to keep performing to be valued. Though she never named it at the time, her behavior was driven by a familiar saboteur: the **Hyper-Achiever,** the belief that worth is measured by external success, not inner fulfillment.

Amanda missed opportunities to pursue roles that truly lit her up, not because she lacked the skills, but because she was emotionally drained by the roles she felt obligated to maintain.

In one of our coaching sessions, I asked her, *"When you hear someone say, you're the CEO of your household, how does that make you feel?"*

She didn't answer with words. She gagged and stuck her tongue out.

That single reaction said more than a paragraph ever could.

And yet, even with that clarity, Amanda still felt drawn to be the 'good wife,' continuing to prioritize others' expectations while leaving her own dreams and ambitions behind.

Margaret: Burnout by Approval

Margaret was a hospital director who spent more time taking care of her team's emotions than leading them. She avoided difficult conversations, took on too many responsibilities, and felt guilty whenever she took a break.

Her saboteur? **The Pleaser.**
A voice that said: *"If they like you, they won't leave you."*
But what it cost her was clarity, boundaries, and credibility with her team.
Eventually, Margaret admitted: *"I don't even know what my leadership style is anymore. I just know I'm tired."*

We all have a **Judge**, and most of us operate with two or three dominant saboteurs. Once you begin to recognize them, you'll start noticing how they shape your choices, especially in your leadership.

Name It To Tame It

Recognize the voice. Reclaim your power.

When your inner critic starts speaking, pause and ask yourself:

- What is this voice really saying?
- Is this truth? Or is it fear?
- Which saboteur is at work here?

Once you identify the saboteur, *name it*. Give it a personality. Turn it into something you can *see*, not something you *are*.

✅ *"That's my Judge again—never satisfied."*

✅ *"Sounds like Taskmaster Tina is back, demanding perfection.*

✅ *"Ah, there's Silent Sam telling me to stay quiet and not take up space."*

What would it look like to *respond* to that voice instead of obeying it?

Naming it gives you distance, and in that space, you reclaim your power to choose.

The High Cost of Unchecked Inner Critics

The saboteurs don't just impact *you*.

They affect how you communicate.

How you handle stress.

How you build trust—or erode it—with your team.

They affect relationships at home, your energy levels, your sense of purpose.

Here are some of the costs I've seen again and again in clients, and, yes, in myself too:

- Emotional burnout disguised as 'being productive'
- Missed promotions from staying silent in meetings
- Underperforming teams because conflict was avoided
- Relationships strained by the pressure to be "on" all the time
- Dreams deferred out of fear of looking selfish or foolish

Can you see yourself in any of these?

Sometimes the saboteur whispers:

"You're doing the right thing by staying quiet."
But the cost is your voice.

"You're being a good leader by taking it all on."
But the cost is your health.

"Don't apply yet. You're not ready."
But the cost is your next opportunity.

Reflection: What Has It Cost You?

Let's pause and take stock.

Use these prompts to gently assess where your inner critic and saboteurs may be running the show, and what it's costing you.

- What's one opportunity you didn't pursue because of self-doubt?
- What feedback or comment still echoes in your mind even years later?
- Which saboteurs sound familiar to you?
  (See list above. Circle or highlight the ones that show up in your thoughts or behaviors.)
- What's the emotional cost of trying to prove, please, or perfect?
- What relationships, roles, or risks have you avoided because of fear or criticism?
- What would be possible if your inner critic wasn't in control?

You are not your saboteurs.
You are not your worst day, your harshest critic, or the role you've been assigned.
You have the power to rewrite the script, even if it's one you've followed for years.

In the next chapter, we'll explore how to transform your inner dialogue, set healthy boundaries, and begin the work of rewriting the script. You'll step fully into the leader you're meant to be, equipped with practical, transformative tools to guide you along the way.

CHAPTER 3

CHAPTER 3

Shifting the Narrative

"When you name your inner critic, you reduce her power.
When you act in spite of her, you take it all away."

The inner critic may be loud—but she doesn't have to be in charge.

By now, you've identified how she speaks and what she costs you. But awareness is only the beginning. This chapter is about writing a new narrative that reflects who you are becoming, not who your saboteurs say you are.

Rewriting the Inner Dialogue

The inner critic thrives on repetition.
She tells the same story over and over:

- You're not ready.
- You'll mess it up.
- You need to be more like someone else.

The antidote isn't denial. It's deliberate narrative rewiring.

"This isn't who I am. It's what I've been taught to believe."
"This voice is fear, not fact."
"What else could be true?"

My Story: From Silencing Muffled Michelle to Empowered Michelle

As I shared earlier, my childhood programming taught me to be silent, obedient, and composed. To only speak when it was safe. To only share what wouldn't rock the boat.

But in leadership, as in real life, you don't always get safe spaces.

Twice in my career, in two different hospital systems, I experienced something devastating: staff members I trusted—people I believed had integrity and a shared commitment to patient safety—falsified medical records. Both of these situations resulted in a fatality. And both led to terminations of my frontline staff.

In the first system, I was supported. The CEO, the CNO, and the senior team gave us space to grieve for the family who lost someone, for the team that witnessed it, and for ourselves. I didn't have to wear the mask of strength. I could be real. The voice that usually told me to stay quiet loosened its grip. You can hardly begin to imagine the devastation of this event, let alone the pressure of having to discuss the "factual" occurrences that took place on my team's watch and mine.

The other staff members also grieved. How could a member of 'our team' do something so egregious? The staff mourned for their unit, their reputation, and the family left behind. Trust was broken, and my team and I had to work on rebuilding trust from within.

But in the second system, the culture was colder. More corporate. I remember being asked by a regional executive who had flown in for the 'deep dive' review: *"If your family member was admitted to this unit, would you feel confident they'd receive safe care?"*

All eyes were on me: the CEO, corporate executives, directors, and my manager. My inner critic whispered, *"Michelle, don't mess this up. Give the politically correct answer."* But for one of the first times in my career, I silenced that voice. She didn't belong in the boardroom with these people. I knew my response might not be what they wanted to hear. Those moments of internal dialogue felt like hours, but finally, I spoke.

And I spoke the truth I had once been afraid to say: *"I would not want my family member admitted here right now."*

That moment became a turning point.

It was one of the most powerful moments in my leadership journey, not because of the outcome, but because of what happened inside me. I was no longer listening to *Muffled Michelle,* the voice of my inner critic who feared being too emotional, too outspoken, too real. I had confronted her, called her out.

And I was freed by my authentic answer.

Even though I paid a price—a shift in how some corporate leaders viewed me, questions about my place in the system—I also gained something far more important:

- A department that got back on track with safety.
- A team that started speaking up again.
- Engagement scores that dipped, then rose, because trust was being rebuilt, not with perfection, but with honesty.
- And corporate leaders who didn't respect my answer

Three out of four wins. I didn't allow the inner critic to return and cloud my judgment. Instead, I stood firm, proud of the truth I had shared and the impact it had. What followed in the next year was a testament to that honesty; it transformed the unit in remarkable ways.

The more I quieted my inner critic, the more others found their authentic voice too.

From Inner Truth to Outer Insight: The Role of Feedback

Speaking my truth in that moment—owning my leadership voice despite the risk—was a pivotal shift in my narrative. It also transformed how I view feedback.

Yes, some may have perceived me as too emotional. After all, a life had been lost due to falsified documentation. But there was nothing I could or would have changed about how I responded.

To accept that feedback, to water myself down or apologize for my authenticity, would have been to betray the leader I knew I needed to be in that moment.

What was the alternative? Stay silent? Pretend nothing had happened? Sweep the truth under the rug?

That wasn't an option. Not for the staff. Not for our patients. Not for the culture we needed to rebuild.

We had work to do, and I was both willing and ready to lead that journey with courage, with conviction, and without compromising who I am. Because once you've faced your inner critic in those pivotal moments, the next challenge is learning how to process feedback without giving her a way back in. This next section will show you how.

What Is Feedback, Really?

The inner critic often twists feedback into fear. But feedback, when approached with clarity, can become a mirror for growth, not a hammer of shame.

To me, feedback is a way to externally validate your contributions, your leadership style, and your impact. It can come through:

- 360-degree evaluations
- Staff comments
- Employee engagement surveys

- Casual observations from colleagues
- Honest conversations with friends and family

True feedback should never be based on fear.

Any time you receive feedback, pause. Reflect.

- What is the truth here?
- Are there patterns or themes?
- Does everyone see me this way?
- And most importantly, can I do something about it?

If the answer is yes, do something about it. See feedback as an invitation. And when you release your inner critic from the driver's seat, you can hear that invitation with more clarity, less judgment, and greater curiosity.

Julie: Facing the Camera and Her Inner Critic

Take my client, Julie. She was growing into a seasoned thought leader in her industry. And part of that growth required putting herself out there, writing articles, offering intellectual commentary, speaking at workshops, and yes, showing up confidently in front of a camera or on Zoom.

Zoom? Oh, those dreaded Zoom meetings.

In one of our coaching sessions, I asked, *"Julie, did you watch the recording of your talk? What did you learn from seeing yourself on screen?"*

She looked at me like I had two heads. *"I didn't watch it,"* she said. *"I can't. I'm too afraid."*

As an accredited coach, I knew we had just stumbled onto something important.

"Tell me more about that," I said. *"What makes it so hard to watch yourself on video?"*

Julie described it as scary. She was afraid she'd see every imperfection, every filler word like "um," every awkward pause, every unpolished sentence. She worried about her voice, her appearance, whether her message landed, whether her facial expressions were awkward, whether she came across as unsure. The fear wasn't just about performance; it was about visibility.

Her inner critic whispered: *You're not polished enough. You're not experienced enough. You're not good enough.*

I asked her, "*So how do you plan to grow as a speaker if you can't observe yourself in action?*"

She laughed and said, "*I guess I don't.*"

That moment revealed a limiting belief that was stalling her growth. Her fear of seeing her flaws, confirming that inner critic's judgment, was stronger than her willingness to evolve.

So I offered something simple. "*How about we watch the video together?*"

She hesitated, but agreed. And we did.

Afterward, I asked her what she noticed.

To her surprise, the experience wasn't nearly as daunting as she had imagined. She recognized areas for improvement, of course, but, more importantly, she noticed what she did well. After I shared my feedback, we celebrated what was strong, what was courageous, and what was evolving.

The meaningful moment?

Julie confronted her fear. She challenged the belief that was holding her back. She saw that the inner critic's opinion wasn't truth—it was unexamined. And with that, she stepped into her next-level self.

We now laugh about that video moment. But it marked the beginning of her owning her presence, not avoiding it.

From Awareness to Empowerment: Tools to Reclaim Your Voice

Whether it's in a boardroom, a Zoom meeting, or during a deeply personal decision, the inner critic always seems to find a way to appear. But you've also witnessed the power that comes from standing up to her, choosing courage over fear, honesty over hesitation.

Moments like mine and Julie's, remind us that while fear and self-doubt may never disappear entirely, they can lose their grip. But this kind of shift doesn't happen by accident. It takes intention. Practice. And the right tools.

If you're ready to quiet the critic and reclaim your confidence, these simple, powerful strategies will help you start rewriting the script.

Tools for Reframing the Inner Critic

Confronting the inner critic isn't about silencing her completely; it's about recognizing her voice, understanding where she comes from, and choosing a more authentic narrative.

▶ Mindfulness Moments
Pause and observe your thoughts without judgment. When your inner critic speaks, ask yourself:
Who is talking right now?
Is this thought helpful or harmful?
What is this fear trying to protect?

Mindfulness creates a gap between the critic's voice and your true self, giving you space to choose your response.

▶ Name & Reframe Technique
This approach empowers you to see your inner critic as a separate voice—not your truth.
Name it: Give your critic a persona to externalize it.
Reframe it: Replace self-limiting beliefs with empowering, authentic narratives.

▶ Thought-Stopping Techniques
When self-judgment creeps in, interrupt it decisively:
Say: "*Not today.*"
Visualize a stop sign.
Write down what it says, then cross it out.

These simple actions help you regain control of your mental space.

▶ Compassionate Reframing & Affirmations
Shift from criticism to compassion. Remind yourself:
"I'm still learning, and that's allowed."
"My value doesn't depend on perfection."
"I can be powerful and still have emotions."

▶ The Boundary Audit

In addition to these mindset tools, I developed the **Boundary Audit**, a structured tool for identifying where your time, energy, and decision-making power might be leaking to obligations instead of being aligned.

The Boundary Audit
- **List all your commitments and roles.**
- **Color-code by emotional weight:**
  - 🔴 Red for resentment
  - 🟡 Yellow for uncertainty
  - 🟢 Green for energy and alignment
- **Reflect:** Where are you over-giving? Where are you thriving?
- **Action:** Choose one red task to reframe, delegate, or release.

The Boundary Audit is a visual map of your energy, revealing where you need to set new boundaries to honor your well-being and authentic leadership.

Amanda: Reclaiming Her Ambition by Naming Her Critic

Let's come back to my client Amanda, the high-achieving perfectionist who once paused coaching because of a deep internal conflict between career and family.

Amanda always wanted to work outside the home, but she also felt immense pressure to be the perfect wife and mother. That pressure became paralyzing. Eventually, she paused our sessions. She wasn't ready, not because she lacked the skill or ambition, but because her inner critic was still running the show.

Yet, like many of my clients, Amanda knew the door to coaching was always open. Months later, she came back.

This time, we didn't just talk about her goals; we examined what had been holding her back. Her inner critic.

I asked her to name it. She laughed nervously and said, *"Amazing Amanda."*

But Amazing Amanda didn't feel amazing. She felt tired. Tired of the push and pull between what she wanted and what she thought she was *supposed* to want.

We got to work. We looked at the messages she'd internalized:

- From her mother who had stayed home full time.
- From church friends who believed that daycare meant "someone else was raising your kids."
- From comments that subtly, or not-so-subtly, invalidated her professional ambition.

We explored how those messages shaped her beliefs, and how to separate inherited values from her own.

Then we turned to her goals.

Amanda began mapping out a career path that honored both her identity and her family life. Within six months, she was working part-time in a laboratory, with the option to transition to full-time once her youngest entered first grade.

She felt like a new person.

In Amanda's journey, we used a powerful technique called **Name & Reframe**, a practice with deep roots in psychology and coaching. The idea of naming the inner critic and reframing its messages isn't new. It stems from the work of Hal and Sidra Stone, who pioneered *Voice Dialogue* to help people engage with different parts of themselves, including the inner critic. It also draws on the reframing practices at the heart of Cognitive Behavioral Therapy (CBT), developed by Aaron Beck and Albert Ellis in the 1960s. More recently, Shirzad Chamine introduced the concept of "Saboteurs" in *Positive Intelligence*, encouraging people to name and challenge the critical voices in their minds.

For Amanda, this meant calling her inner critic "Amazing Amanda" and recognizing that the pressure to be the perfect wife, mother, and leader wasn't really coming from her. It was a legacy of family expectations and cultural messaging that had shaped her beliefs but didn't align with her real ambitions. In our work together, we explored those messages and separated what she wanted from what she thought she was supposed to want. This simple but transformative process gave her the clarity and courage to reclaim her ambition on her own terms.

Naming her inner critic, uncovering her emotional triggers, and defining what healthy balance meant for her gave Amanda more than clarity—it gave her freedom.

Margaret: Rebuilding Boundaries and Reclaiming Leadership

Margaret was a hospital director adored by her team, but not in a way that supported strong leadership. She was approachable, accommodating, and always available. She remembered birthdays, brought cupcakes, and often stayed late to help others finish their work.

But the cost? She avoided hard conversations. She said *"yes"* when she meant *"not now."* And over time, her team respected her kindness, but questioned her authority. Her saboteur, the **Pleaser**, ran the show. Its voice whispered: *"If they like you, they won't leave you."*

Margaret was burning out, emotionally, mentally, even physically. So we introduced a simple but powerful tool: the **Boundary Audit**.

We made a list of all the places she was giving away her time, energy, and decision-making power to obligations rather than aligning them with her true self. We color-coded tasks by emotional weight: red for resentment; yellow for uncertainty; green for energizing.

Most of her calendar was red. Then came the real work: learning to say **"no"** without apology, and **"yes"** with intention.

We built scripts for conversations she had been avoiding:

- Delegating without guilt
- Holding staff accountable with kindness, not fear
- Protecting her calendar without overexplaining

With every boundary Margaret reinforced, her confidence grew. Her team began stepping up more because they now knew where she stood. Respect didn't fade. It deepened.

The turning point?

One Friday afternoon, after yet another last-minute request from a team member who had a habit of pushing limits, Margaret paused and said calmly: *"I trust you'll be able to handle that. I'll follow up with you next week."*

And then she left on time.

That weekend, she didn't bring her laptop home. She went hiking with her sister. And when she returned Monday morning, she told me:

"That one sentence changed how I see myself. I'm no longer managing approval. I'm leading."

You don't have to banish your inner critic.
You just need to change how you respond.

Reflection Practice: Build Your Reframing Muscle

At the end of each day, ask yourself:

* When did my critic show up today?
* What did I choose to believe instead?
* What would I tell a friend who felt the same way?

A growth mindset isn't about blind positivity.
It's about believing you're worthy of change.

Reflection: Rewrite the Narrative

* What belief do I need to let go of in order to grow?
* When have I let feedback define me instead of develop me?
* What would change if I treated myself like someone worth investing in?

Looking Ahead: The Work of Resilience

You've named your inner critic. You've set boundaries. You've started rewriting the script.

But leadership isn't just about what you say no to; it's about how you show up when things get hard.

In Chapter 4, we'll explore what it means to build true resilience, not the kind that hides exhaustion behind a brave face, but the kind that expands your capacity to recover, reset, and rise.

Because courage isn't about never struggling. It's about learning how to respond when you do, and still move forward with clarity, confidence, and conviction.

CHAPTER 4

CHAPTER 4:

Building Resilience

"Every setback is a signal, not of failure,
but of your readiness to rise"

Resilience isn't just about bouncing back; it's about pushing forward with clarity, purpose, and strength forged through adversity. For leaders, resilience isn't optional. It's foundational. It shapes how we lead in times of uncertainty. It guides how we respond when the inner critic whispers that we're not enough. And it determines how we keep moving forward—even in the presence of fear.

In this chapter, we'll explore how to cultivate it.

What Is Resilience Really?

Resilience isn't perfection. It's not emotional armor. And it's not pushing through at all costs.

Resilience is your ability to:

- Face discomfort without shutting down
- Recover from self-doubt with perspective
- Stay grounded in your values when external feedback or outcomes shift
- Choose growth over retreat

Amanda: Redefining Strength

When Amanda first joined my coaching program, she thought resilience meant keeping everyone happy while suppressing her own ambition. But naming her inner critic, "Amazing Amanda", gave her language for the internal battle she was fighting.

Over time, she learned that honoring her calling was not selfish, it was essential. By understanding the *why* behind her guilt, and challenging it through reflection, she created a new version of resilience: one built on aligned choices, not people-pleasing.

Today, Amanda continues to thrive professionally while maintaining boundaries with compassion. Her resilience is rooted in balance and integration, not burnout.

Margaret: Boundaries as a Catalyst

Margaret's resilience journey began when she realized burnout wasn't just physical; it was a lack of clarity. By using the Boundary Audit tool, she stopped over-functioning for others and started leading with intention.

With each new boundary she set, her energy, confidence, and presence grew. She didn't stop caring; she just stopped carrying everything.

Her resilience didn't come from being less emotional. It came from being more honest about what she needed.

Julie: Confidence Through Exposure

Julie's turning point came when she confronted her fear of visibility. Watching herself on video was terrifying at first, but by naming her fears and discovering that the reality was far kinder than her inner critic's script, she reclaimed her power.

Now, each Zoom meeting, each recorded workshop, becomes an opportunity to practice—not prove. Her resilience is built through repetition and recovery.

Resilience doesn't mean eliminating the inner critic. It means outlasting her.

Me: Resilience in Leadership

There were moments in my career when I believed strength meant never revealing pain. However, I came to realize that true leadership emerged when I made room for vulnerability, faced up to difficult questions, and confronted uncomfortable truths.

Resilience doesn't mean you don't get knocked down.
It means you know how to stand up, realign,
and lead forward without losing yourself.

How to Build Everyday Resilience

While stories can inspire us, resilience is built into the daily choices we make. Here are practical ways you can integrate resilience into your leadership rhythm:

- **Build in Recovery Time**
  Resilience isn't about pushing on endlessly. It's about knowing when to pause. Just like athletes build rest into their training plans, resilient leaders schedule mental recovery, whether it's a walk, deep breathing between meetings, or even 15 minutes of quiet.
- **Establish a Reflective Practice**
  Amanda started journaling for 10 minutes each night, not about what she got done, but how she felt and what her critic said that day. Naming the thought helped her shift it the next time it appeared.
- **Use a Support Sounding Board**
  Margaret didn't just audit her boundaries; she practiced expressing her new scripts with a trusted peer first. Rehearsal builds confidence before pressure hits.
- **Anchor Your Actions to Your Values**
  When I felt emotionally vulnerable after leading through a crisis, I went back to my core values: authenticity, safety, clarity. They became my filter for decisions, not public opinion.

- **Celebrate Small Wins**
Julie didn't wait until her keynote was flawless to celebrate. She acknowledged the courage it took to rewatch her first Zoom recording. That was the win. Resilience grows from the moment you try again.

Resilience Framework: The 4 R's framework is grounded in trauma informed approach

Before we return to more client stories, let's ground ourselves in a practical framework to build resilience in real time. The 4 R's provide a structure for shifting away from reaction and toward intentional response. These are the tools my clients often use—sometimes without realizing it—to take back control from their inner critic and move forward with clarity. The 4 R's help you to disrupt your inner critic and re-center yourself:

1. Recognize
Pay attention to your physical and emotional cues. When are you triggered? What situations cause your inner critic to speak up? Awareness is always the first step.

2. Reflect
Ask yourself:

- What story am I telling myself right now?
- Is this story rooted in truth or fear?
- What past experiences might be influencing my reaction?

3. Reframe
Shift from judgment to curiosity:

- What else could be true?
- How would I speak to a friend in this situation?
- What strength can I lead with instead?

4. Respond
Take one bold, aligned action. Not a perfect action, but a true one. One that brings you closer to your values and your vision, not your saboteur's script.

The SOAR Model: A Framework for Resilient Leadership

You've seen how Amanda, Margaret, Julie, and I each rebuilt trust in ourselves through adversity. But how do we make that kind of inner growth sustainable? How do we move from isolated breakthroughs to a consistent leadership rhythm grounded in reflection, action, and alignment?

That's where the SOAR Model comes in. This is a proven process I designed not just to help leaders recover, but to grow and evolve—again and again. Resilience isn't about sidestepping hardship; it's about weaving your setbacks into your journey of growth. The SOAR Model offers a structured, repeatable framework that empowers leaders to anchor themselves in truth, rise above fear, and lead with unwavering strength.

SOAR MODEL OF EMPOWERMENT AND GROWTH

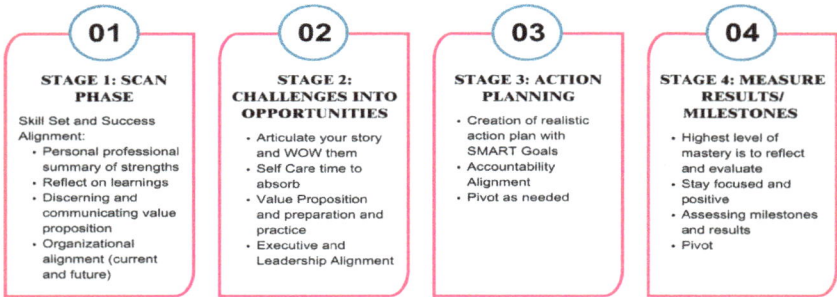

01	02	03	04
STAGE 1: SCAN PHASE	**STAGE 2: CHALLENGES INTO OPPORTUNITIES**	**STAGE 3: ACTION PLANNING**	**STAGE 4: MEASURE RESULTS/ MILESTONES**
Skill Set and Success Alignment: • Personal professional summary of strengths • Reflect on learnings • Discerning and communicating value proposition • Organizational alignment (current and future)	• Articulate your story and WOW them • Self Care time to absorb • Value Proposition and preparation and practice • Executive and Leadership Alignment	• Creation of realistic action plan with SMART Goals • Accountability Alignment • Pivot as needed	• Highest level of mastery is to reflect and evaluate • Stay focused and positive • Assessing milestones and results • Pivot

Here's how it works:

S — Scan

The Scan phase is based on the principle: *'Know thyself to grow thyself.'* More than self-awareness, it's about understanding the internal and external environments in which you live and work. By scanning both, you'll uncover triggers that either align with or challenge your truth. This phase helps you:

- Understand your communication patterns and blind spots.
- Examine your home and work environments: Are your values aligned with the culture around you?
- Recognize warning signs when something feels misaligned or unsafe.

O — Opportunity

Adversity doesn't have to hold you back—it can be the fuel for your next breakthrough. In this phase, you'll reflect on:

- The lessons hidden within your recent challenges
- Outdated beliefs or habits you've released
- Areas where you're being invited to grow, pivot, or expand

A — Action

Resilient leadership is built on clarity, not fear. This phase is about taking intentional steps that align with your authentic self. Ask yourself:

- What daily or weekly actions will move me closer to the leader I want to become?
- What do I need to stop doing to become the balanced woman, bold leader, or whole human being I envision?

R — Results

True resilience celebrates progress, not perfection. In this phase, you'll focus on:

- Measuring what matters most to you
- Tracking personal, relational, and professional wins
- Pausing to acknowledge how far you've come, because growth without celebration feels like survival, not strength

The SOAR Model isn't just a framework; it's a mindset, a movement, and a powerful way to lead with purpose. It reminds us that setbacks aren't failures; they're opportunities to grow and evolve.

SOARing isn't about avoiding fear; it's about embracing growth, even in the face of challenges.

You can start exploring the SOAR approach today by reflecting on the following questions:

- When was the last time I overcame a challenge I didn't think I could handle?
- What did I discover about myself in the process?
- Which of my values guided me through it?
- What would resilience look like in a current struggle I'm facing?
- What clear actions can I take to grow, strategize, or get back on track?

- When was the last time I celebrated a milestone? How did that make me feel?

If you're ready to dive deeper into the full SOAR experience, exploring Scan, Opportunity, Action, and Results in more depth, reach out to me directly at Michelle@MichelleDestefano.coach. I'd love to guide you on this transformative journey.

Linking Resilience to Real-World Results

The SOAR Model isn't just a tool for self-reflection; it's a strategic framework that delivers tangible business outcomes. Leaders who consistently reflect, adapt, and act in alignment with their values are better equipped to:

- Make faster, value-driven decisions under pressure
- Build cultures where people feel safe to speak up and solve problems
- Recover quickly from setbacks without losing momentum
- Align their leadership presence with organizational performance metrics

Leading through SOAR helps you to create structure, meaning, and measurable impact in the midst of the chaos of modern life.

Tangible results when the SOAR model is put into practice:

- **Improved patient safety**, because resilient leaders stay grounded and make sound decisions under pressure
- **Greater team engagement**, due to a culture of psychological safety where staff feel seen and heard
- **Stronger adaptability**, especially during change initiatives, restructuring, or crisis events
- **Better business outcomes**, including lower employee turnover, higher satisfaction, and sustainable performance

My Own Resilience Story: Leading Through Tragedy with the SOAR Strategy

One of the pivotal moments in my leadership journey came in the aftermath of tragedy. It was a time when I had to reclaim my voice amid loss, scrutiny, and emotional upheaval. It was a test not only of my role, but of my resilience.

A tragic patient safety event had occurred. Despite our efforts to build a culture of accountability and safety, policies, safety precautions, and staff competencies were not yet ingrained. The result was that a patient died under our care. The loss was devastating and the emotional weight across the unit was immeasurable.

Here's how the SOAR model was applied to this situation:

S — Scan

This is where we often spend most time as leaders, especially in times of uncertainty or crisis. For me, this phase wasn't just about assessing the events happening around me; it was about confronting myself.

As I scanned the landscape of my leadership, I began to see the cracks in the culture we were trying to build. It wasn't that I hadn't invested in the team or communicated the vision; it was that not everyone had embraced it. That realization was painful, but liberating. It taught me that culture isn't created by one leader alone—it requires shared ownership.

I was aware of my leadership style: persevering, strategic, authentic. But during this scan phase, I came to understand that my messaging had to be sharper and more intentional. I had to communicate with absolute clarity and unwavering conviction.

I also had to face a truth I hadn't wanted to acknowledge: this environment might not be the right fit for the leadership style I was trying to embody.

My team was hurting. They were shaken, fearful, disappointed, and anxious. I didn't just scan my inner world, I scanned theirs. I rearranged my calendar, restructured my leadership team and became a consistent, visible presence in the unit, not just as an executive, but as a steady, reliable leader. The culture needed to heal, and I couldn't delegate that. I had to model it.

I also had to assess my external environment; I faced criticism from corporate leadership for being "too emotional." But I stood firm, refusing to apologize for my humanity. When asked if I would admit my own family member to that unit, I paused, took a breath, and answered truthfully:

"Not at this time."

That moment, as painful as it was, marked a turning point. It became the intersection of inner clarity and external courage—the exact place where empowered leadership begins.

O — Opportunity

The opportunity phase, the second critical phase in the SOAR framework, is about letting go of what no longer serves us to make room for something new to emerge.

In those early days of navigating the aftermath, I realized the goal wasn't just to fix what had failed; it was to reimagine what was possible.

The rawness of the situation revealed truths that had been buried under years of habit and complacency. It was an invitation to ask deeper questions:

- What does true safety look like for patients and staff?
- How can we lead with integrity when the system feels broken?
- How can we make compassion visible, through both words and daily actions?

Rather than treating this as an ending, I chose to seize the opportunity: to build a better department grounded in transparency, integrity, and healing.

Our goal was not just to stabilize the situation; it was to rise stronger. I identified a new path where staff would feel empowered, where systems would be fortified, and where the culture would reflect the values we claimed to hold.

But this opportunity doesn't just happen by itself. It requires courage to name what's not working and to let go of what no longer aligns. It requires leaders to model the very behaviors we expect from our teams. It requires a shift in mindset: from surviving to innovating.

In this phase, I asked myself and my team:

- What small, daily actions do we need to take to build trust and hope?
- How do we make room for new voices to be heard?
- What's the first courageous step we can take together?

The answers weren't always immediately obvious. But the act of asking, and of choosing to see opportunity in the cracks, became our path forward.

A — Action

We didn't wait. We acted.

- **We reintroduced daily safety huddles** at the start of every shift to ensure staff felt seen, heard, and supported.
- **We established transparent communication channels** to rebuild trust and allow information to be shared openly.
- **We increased leadership presence** through purposeful rounding and active, steady support.
- **We launched 360-degree feedback cycles** to gather honest insights and empower continuous growth.
- **We provided coaching and grief counseling resources** to support emotional healing and foster resilience.

These initiatives weren't performative gestures; they were purposeful steps toward a commitment to healing and growth.

I communicated the plan clearly to the CEO and executive leadership. My team and I kept the staff informed every step of the way, providing them with feedback and follow-up information. This wasn't damage control; it was a blueprint for healing and change.

R — Results

One year later, we saw the tangible rewards of the transformation. We measured what mattered. We pivoted when things declined and celebrated when actions created change in results, thinking, and behaviors:

- Employee engagement doubled.
- Staff retention increased significantly.
- Patient safety checks became routine and team-led.
- The culture shifted from reactive to proactive. And trust returned.

To SOAR.
Not to fly above adversity but to rise through it,
with courage, strategy, integrity and resilience.

From Inner Work to Outer Impact

Resilience isn't just a personal quality. It shows up in how we lead, how we make decisions under pressure, and how we adapt within complex systems. The leaders who drive lasting change aren't just intelligent or charismatic; they're rooted, reflective, and real. Because the goal isn't to eliminate discomfort. It's to expand your capacity to lead through it.

In Chapter 5, we'll move from resilience to empowerment. What if your inner critic became your inner coach? What if the voice that once held you back could become the one that helps you rise? We'll explore how to rewrite that new narrative, through habits, mindset shifts, and real-life leadership moments from Amanda, Margaret, Julie, and my own journey. This is where self-trust meets decisive leadership, and where transformation truly begins.

CHAPTER 5

CHAPTER 5

Leadership Lessons for Empowerment

"Setbacks aren't stop signs; they're redirections to something greater than you imagined."

From Disruption to Reinvention: A Journey of Empowered Leadership

It began like any other morning. I arrived at 6:30 AM to make rounds, just as I always had: checking on progress in the units, connecting with the staff, and ensuring the culture we had worked so hard to build was thriving.

But that day, something felt different.

I had heard whispers that changes might be coming. Still, I showed up with integrity, believing in what we were building and in the team I led. I believed, despite quiet doubts, that I would remain. Because that's what authentic, committed leadership looks like.

Until I heard the words:
"We're going in a different direction."

In the corporate world, this phrase is often a polished way of saying you're no longer needed, not because of misconduct or poor performance, but because of a decision that changes the course of everything. For me, it meant I was let go, not fired, with a severance package to soften the blow.

It's a phrase that sounds neutral, even kind, but it lands like a punch to the gut. It wasn't just my position that was lost; it felt like an erasure of the years I had poured into shaping culture, building trust, and leading transformation. But this was the moment that changed everything:

Instead of letting that experience define me, I chose to redefine it.

The Coaching That Changed Everything

I turned to an executive coach, seeking guidance to regain clarity and uncover the purpose hidden within the pain. Together, we did what I now help others achieve—we mapped out the next chapter with honesty, strategy, and unwavering courage. I began to own my leadership legacy, not by holding onto the past, but by recognizing the transferable value of what I had already accomplished.

But let me be clear: I didn't get there overnight. I cried. I mourned. There were days I felt completely lost, when my grief was so heavy I didn't know how to move forward. Staff reached out, checking in:

"Are you okay?"

I appreciated their concern, but it reminded me just how visible my pain had become. I gave myself space to breathe, to feel the weight of what had happened. But soon, I channeled that grief into action. I thought I had something to prove. I was determined to show everyone that I could be a Chief Nursing Officer again, maybe not for myself, but for them. For my peers. For the people who doubted I could recover. It wasn't the most pragmatic way to view my world or to empower myself, but it was my first reaction. My gut response was:

"I'll prove them wrong."

I applied for various roles, including CNO positions. I went on-site for interviews, ready to convince myself and everyone else that I still belonged at the top. But what I found were the same stories, wrapped in new wallpaper: recycled environments and empty recruitment promises. I met leaders, former CNOs who had "moved up" to COO roles. They called themselves "recovering CNOs," as if that label somehow gave them an identity.

Recovering? Recovering from what? It felt disempowering. Their energy said it all: they weren't thriving; they were surviving. I realized this wasn't the life I wanted. I wasn't recovering; I was releasing. I was releasing the need to prove myself to anyone else. I was releasing the idea that my worth was tied to a title or a particular organization. I was releasing the belief that leadership meant sacrificing my voice and vision for someone else's agenda.

During that time, I came to a profound realization: I could reinvent myself. I could take charge of my own story. I could choose to lead differently, to impact not just one organization, but many. I wanted to be an innovator. A thought leader. Someone who used her voice, her lived experiences, and her passion to help others navigate change.

But before I could get there, I had to grieve. I had to feel the weight of everything I'd lost, and everything I still wanted to create. I had to release the past to step into the future.

And I did.

That moment didn't mark the end of my leadership. It marked the beginning of my reinvention. Eventually, I was offered a CNO position at a respected system. But through the internal work I had done and the unwavering support of my executive coach, I experienced my most transformative moment yet. I realized I had already proven myself. I didn't need another title to validate my worth. In that moment, I chose freedom. I chose to reinvent myself, and I felt more empowered and aligned than ever before.

Empowerment Begins When You Name the Fear: Paula's Story

Empowerment doesn't always begin with action. Sometimes, it starts by *naming* what we've been too afraid to admit.

Paula reached out for a discovery call during a season of immense pressure.

She was completing her doctorate while stepping into a new position that had no clearly defined objectives. It had emerged following a restructuring, and even senior leaders were unsure how to navigate the change, let alone lead others through it.

When I asked her where the anxiety was coming from, she looked visibly distressed. She couldn't articulate the next step because her inner critic had hijacked the moment.

I gently said, *"Name it. Define it. What's causing the most stress?"*

Without hesitation, she blurted out:
"I'm afraid of losing my job."

In that moment, her shoulders dropped. Her face softened.
"I feel better just saying that out loud," she admitted.

That was her turning point. Once she named the fear, it no longer controlled her. From there, she began shifting into an empowerment mindset: updating her resume, clarifying her evolving role, and staying alert to change.

Empowerment doesn't mean ignoring fear. It means facing it, naming it, and acting anyway.

Empowerment Multiplied: Joan's Story

Joan had worked in the same organization since graduating nursing school. She worked her way through the ranks and was seen as a rising star. But one day, her department was abruptly shut down, not because of poor leadership, but due to financial restructuring driven by system-wide decisions outside of her control.

She was devastated. "What do I do now?" she asked.

That's when she joined my Career Accelerator Program. Together, we:

• Rewrote her leadership narrative, documenting her successes and reclaiming her voice.

- Mapped out her next chapter, focusing on clarity, vision, and self-definition.
- Explored what does and does not define a leader.

Less than a year later, Joan stepped into a new role in an organization that truly valued her leadership. Within another year, she was promoted.

What Is Empowerment Really?

Empowerment isn't a buzzword. It's not about slogans or surface-level motivation.
Empowerment is the practice of reclaiming your leadership voice, especially in the aftermath of disruption.

Empowerment is…

- Clarity: Knowing who you are beyond your role
- Courage: Choosing to move forward, even when the path isn't clear
- Agency: Taking ownership of what you want to create next
- Perspective: Recognizing that one moment doesn't define your entire story
- Support: Surrounding yourself with those who will remind you of your worth

Empowerment is not…

- Dependent on a title or organization.
- About pretending everything is okay when it's not.
- A solo journey with no roadmap.

Empowered Leaders Empower Others

Empowerment doesn't stop with you. In fact, the true test of your leadership is how many others rise with you, not just in performance, but in purpose.

As leaders, we're responsible for:

- Creating psychological safety so our teams feel seen and heard.
- Helping staff uncover their "why": what drives them, excites them, and fuels their best work.
- Coaching our team through their own inner critic moments, not with judgment, but with curiosity and encouragement.
- Being the kind of leader who *grows leaders,* not one who just manages staff.

Team Empowerment Practices

Ask Deeper Questions
In leadership sessions, go beyond metrics. Ask:
"What part of your work excites you most?"
"Where do you want to grow next?"
"What would make your role more meaningful?"

Name Your Strengths
Most people underestimate themselves. Reflect back what you see:
"You are good at remaining calm in chaos."
"Your insight during that meeting shifted the entire discussion."

Invite Them Into the Process
When leading change, ask:
"What do you think would make this better?"
"If you were leading this, where would you start?"

Celebrate Becoming, Not Just Achieving
Recognize effort, resilience, learning, and voice, not just end results.

The Empowered Leader's Toolkit

If you're ready to take on the mantle of empowered leadership, here are five practices to begin today:

1. **Rewrite Your Story**
   List your key accomplishments, not just outcomes, but the leadership strengths you used to get there.

2. **Define What's Next**
   Journal: "*If nothing held me back, what would my leadership legacy be?*"

3. **Audit Your Voice**
   Listen to your inner dialogue. Does it uplift or diminish you? Begin replacing fear with truth.

4. **Reconnect with Mentors or Coaches**
   You don't have to figure this out alone. Strategic guidance accelerates clarity.

5. **Expand Your Impact**
   Ask: "*Where else could I lead with the value I bring?*" Sometimes the next chapter is *bigger* than the one before.

Reflection Questions

1. When have you experienced a disruption in your career that made you question your identity as a leader? What did you learn from it?

2. What unspoken fears may be influencing your leadership decisions?

3. How would your leadership change if your inner dialogue shifted from criticism to empowerment?

4. What strengths or successes have you minimized that deserve to be acknowledged and celebrated?

5. How are you actively helping your team members discover their purpose and grow into their full potential?

6. Who do you turn to for clarity and support when navigating uncertainty, and how might you strengthen that circle?

7. What's one bold, empowering action you can take this week to move closer to the next version of your leadership legacy?

Your legacy isn't built by avoiding hard moments. It's built from what you make of them, and bringing others along with you.

Reinvention doesn't happen in isolation. I've discovered that while personal courage and clarity are essential, they're only part of the journey. True empowerment is sustained—and magnified—by support and community.

I didn't reach my turning point alone. My executive coach was my guide, my mirror, and my truth-teller. As I worked through my fears and redefined my leadership identity, I also discovered the power of my own inner coach, a voice that began to quiet the relentless inner critic.

That combination—the external guidance from my coach and the internal courage to rewrite my story—became the foundation of my personal empowerment. The community I had built around me, friends, colleagues, mentors, became the anchor that steadied me and the springboard that launched me forward.

In the next chapter, we'll explore the vital role of positive influences and reciprocal support in your leadership journey. Because while self-awareness is foundational, it's community and the inner voice we nurture that sustain us when the weight is too heavy to carry alone.

Empowerment isn't a destination; it's a decision.

It begins with telling the truth, especially to yourself. It grows when you take strategic action. And it multiplies when you empower others to rise alongside you.

CHAPTER 6

CHAPTER 6

Strength Through Support and Community

"If your inner critic spoke to your best friend that way, would you let her continue? Then why let her speak to you"

Ultimately, leadership is never a solo act. Even the strongest leaders need a trusted circle—voices that challenge us, hold us accountable, and remind us of our worth when our inner critic grows loud.

The inner critic doesn't just creep into boardrooms and project plans. It follows us into our personal lives, when we're scrolling through photos of an event we weren't invited to, when we're left out of conversations we thought we belonged in, when we wonder:

"What did I do? Why wasn't I enough?"

Mel Robbins shared a moment like this. As she scrolled through social media, seeing friends at an event she wasn't invited to, her inner critic whispered:

"You must have done something wrong."
Her inner coach countered:
"Maybe you didn't. Maybe this just isn't your tribe."

I know that feeling. Many years ago, I was bullied in grade school, excluded, singled out, and made to feel invisible. I had moved past that pain—or so I thought. But recently, I found myself reliving a version of it as an adult.

A "friend" didn't invite me to her birthday gathering. I saw the photos on Facebook; I zoomed in to be sure. My inner critic said:

"You're not enough. You must have done something."
My authentic self said:
"Maybe you didn't. Maybe this just isn't your people."

But it still hurt. I cried on the golf course after this happened. I reached out, vulnerable and honest, only to find that what I thought was friendship wasn't mutual. That was my scan phase—my personal leadership moment outside of work. I realized I didn't need to prove myself or chase a place at a table that wasn't meant for me.

And I also realized this: building a community isn't just about what you receive; it's about what you bring. True support and connection require us to show up as we are, to share openly, and to invest in others. It's an 80/20 balance—yes, you deserve to be surrounded by people who lift you up, but you must also be willing to contribute, to give, and to model the very values you seek.

Mel Robbins touched on this subject in her book *Let Them*. When she wasn't invited to a gathering, she paused to consider: had she been showing up for others? Was she truly invested in the relationships she wanted? Her insight was powerful.

But my story was a little different. Even as I was overlooked, I was showing up to the best of my ability. I had volunteered, despite my busy work schedule, to serve on the Ladies' Golfing Board. I worked tirelessly to bring in sponsors for our big tournaments. I had even planned a gathering for the same "friend" who now was at her gathering without me. I organized December birthday celebrations for those of us born during the holiday season, so we wouldn't be overlooked in the midst of the hustle and bustle. The irony wasn't lost on me.

What stung most was that I had always been described as the inclusive one and the neutral one. The person who made sure everyone felt seen and welcome.

Yet in that moment, I realized: *Let them. Let them have their gathering without me. And let me... let them go.*

In letting them go, I discovered a deeper truth: my inclusiveness didn't mean everyone would include me in return. And that's okay. Because real community isn't built on forced connections, but on shared values and mutual respect.

The Power of Positive Influences

In both personal and professional settings, positive influences can change everything. Supportive communities validate our humanity and challenge us to grow. They become the mirrors that reflect our best selves, and are the safety nets that catch us when we stumble.

In my career journey, my executive coach wasn't just a sounding board. He was a partner in truth-telling, a guide who reminded me that growth requires release. But as I did the work, I also discovered the power of my own inner coach, a voice that quieted my inner critic and encouraged me to see possibilities beyond the pain.

In your professional life, your community might be trusted peers who help you find opportunity in your setbacks, or mentors who model what's possible when you lead with authenticity.

Setting Boundaries with Love and Integrity

Supportive communities also require boundaries, clear agreements about what you're willing to share, where you're willing to invest, and what you need to feel safe. Boundaries aren't walls; they're bridges that protect your energy and allow you to show up fully for those who matter most.

Some helpful tips:

- Communicate expectations openly and listen for alignment.
- Notice which conversations energize you and which deplete you.
- Walk away from circles that erode your confidence or make you question your worth.

Reciprocal Mentorship: Learning and Lifting through Professional Networking

Reciprocal mentorship is a reminder that growth doesn't happen in isolation; it happens when we're connected and committed to lifting others just as they support us. This sense of community, of showing up not just for ourselves, but for those around us, naturally extends to professional networking. Networking isn't simply a tool for career advancement; it's a practice of building trust, sharing wisdom, and amplifying our collective impact.

Networking isn't just about jobs or connections. It's about building trust, sharing wisdom, and gaining support that extends far beyond a single career move.

Let me introduce John, one of my signature clients who embodied this transformation. When John first came to me, he wanted to advance his career. He was driven and knew he had a lot to offer, but like many leaders, he thought that updating his resume was the answer. He believed the right bullet points would unlock his next opportunity.

But we went deeper and soon, John realized that the resume was just one piece of the puzzle. We focused on personal branding, not just what he did, but who he was and how he showed up as a leader. We explored professional networking, both online and in person. And that's where the transformation happened for John.

Networking is often misunderstood. Many leaders I coach, whether they're accelerating their careers by choice or out of necessity, treat networking as a lifeline, something to grab only when they're drowning. But that's not real networking. Real networking is about the 80/20 rule: you show up willing to contribute, to share your wisdom and skills generously, knowing that what you give will return to you many times over.

John mastered this. He wrote a letter to his professional network not about himself, but about how he could solve problems for others, how his skills could make their work easier, their teams stronger. We leveraged his **CliftonStrengths** results to identify his natural talents and position him through the lens of strength-based leadership. This wasn't about bragging; it was about being of service.

And that 20% of effort he put into genuinely marketing himself and his contributions? It paid off in an 80% perception shift. Other leaders began to see John not as another candidate, but as a thought partner, a collaborator, someone they wanted in their circle.

John didn't stop there. He gave back to his professional community, serving his state nursing organization with the same spirit of contribution. He expanded his professional community to healthcare groups beyond nursing. His example taught me, and reminded so many of my clients, that networking isn't a job-hunting tool. It's a lifelong practice that builds a trusted community around you.

So what does networking have to do with the inner critic? Everything. Because when you're surrounded by people who see your strengths, who value your contributions, and who want you to succeed, it's much harder for that critical voice inside you to take center stage. Networking isn't just about opportunity; it's about quieting the inner critic by finding your tribe. It's about creating a circle of support where vulnerability is met with encouragement, and ambition is met with possibility.

This is the magic of reciprocal relationships, where learning and teaching; mentoring and coaching become two sides of the same coin.

Action Steps for Building and Nurturing Your Circle

Here are some ways to start cultivating a strong, supportive leadership community:

Identify Your 3 Key Supporters
Find the people who see you fully and call you forward, those who believe in your potential for growth and aren't afraid to challenge you.

Clarify Your Boundaries
Reflect on which conversations and relationships align with your values and which spaces no longer serve your growth.

Invest in Others' Growth
Offer your insights, your time, or simply your presence. Be the leader who lifts others up as they climb.

Seek Diverse Perspectives
Surround yourself with people who think differently. Growth happens when you're open to new ideas and willing to learn from them.

Embrace Vulnerability
Be willing to share both your struggles and your strengths. True leadership is rooted in authenticity and connection.

Practice Authentic Networking
See networking not as a transactional tool, but as a practice of mutual growth and support. Approach conversations with curiosity and a mindset of contribution. Remember: real networking is about sharing who you are, what you're working toward, and how you can support others along the way.

You don't have to walk this path alone. Your leadership journey will always be stronger and more joyful when you're surrounded by a community that sees and celebrates you.

For me, the lesson was deeply personal. After years of investing in women's groups, volunteering my time, bringing in sponsors, and creating gatherings, I realized that community isn't always defined by the invitations we receive. Sometimes, it's about recognizing when it's time to let others have their space, and giving ourselves permission to move on.

That experience taught me that real community isn't about forced belonging. It's about finding the people who share your values, your energy, and your commitment to showing up fully.

Today, I'm far more intentional about the groups I engage with and the communities I choose to be part of. Before I raise my hand, I make sure my own cup is full, so I'm not pouring from a place of depletion.

That was the moment I finally quieted the inner critic who insisted that more was always better. I learned that more is often just…more, and is not necessarily meaningful or impactful.

And remember leadership isn't just about being supported. It's about becoming the kind of leader who supports others in return, someone who shows up with courage, curiosity, and a willingness to invest in the growth of those around them.

Reflection Questions

1. Who are the 3 key supporters in your life right now? And how do they help you see your strengths?

2. Where might you be holding back from sharing your ideas or insights with your community?

3. How can you reframe networking as a practice of authentic connection and contribution, rather than a transaction?

4. Where in your life have you had to let go of spaces that no longer fit with who you are becoming?

As we close this chapter, remember: your leadership journey is not just about personal growth; it's about how that growth ripples outward. When you find your voice, when you set clear boundaries, and when you show up in authentic relationships and community, you're laying the foundation for leadership that resonates.

Let's turn now to **Chapter 7**, where we'll gather the key takeaways from this book and look ahead. You'll be encouraged to keep silencing your inner critic, to lean into the practices that help you lead with clarity and purpose. You'll see how every moment of growth, no matter how small, translates into greater professional success and a lasting legacy.

Are you ready to take your next step? Let's move forward together.

CHAPTER 7

CHAPTER 7

The Near-Death Experience and Its Lessons

"Your dreams don't need permission from your inner critic; they need commitment from you."

On December 18, 2024—just one day after my birthday—I thought my life was over.

It was a beautiful day in southern Texas. The sun was shining, and I felt an overwhelming sense of gratitude. My business was thriving. Potential clients were reaching out on LinkedIn, and a student nurse from Africa had just thanked me publicly for mentoring her through all the challenges she faced. I felt proud. Settled. Energized.

My husband and I decided to take the afternoon off to play golf.

We were off to a great start. As I drove the cart toward the ladies' tee box, a path I'd taken countless times, the wheels suddenly slipped. The ground gave way, and in one terrifying instant, I found myself still upright but hanging over the edge of a cliff

From his tee box, my husband watched it happen. He thought: She's gone. And honestly? So did I.

I didn't see a gentle stop or a soft landing. I saw a broken back. Massive head trauma. The end of my story, my legacy, and everything I'd worked for. But then… the cart stopped. Miraculously. I didn't have a scratch, only a bruise on my left leg.

The next day, I broke down. I cried and shook as the gravity of what almost happened sank in. But here's what surprised me most:

I don't experience trauma every time I golf at that hole. In fact, I play it almost every week.

Six months later, I watched another golfer crash her cart, this time on the way to the clubhouse. Blood poured down her face. My husband and I, both healthcare professionals, rushed to help. Trauma mode kicked in, calm and instinctive.

Afterward, I asked myself:
Why wasn't I more shaken? Why don't I flinch when I think about my own close call?

The answer was simple:
It wasn't my time.
And I have more to do.

This experience didn't leave me fearful; it left me fiercely focused. On life. On legacy. On you.

It did something else, too: it quieted my inner critic.

Because when you're hanging off a cliff, worrying whether you're good enough becomes irrelevant. Life is too precious to waste on second-guessing. Too short to be held hostage by a voice that was never yours to begin with.

I won't pretend my inner critic disappeared forever. But that day, she lost her power. And I decided that if I was given another chance, I would not spend it playing small.

In the next chapter, we'll put all of this together, and map out how you can step forward with the same clarity, confidence, and courage.

CHAPTER 8

CHAPTER 8

Putting It All Together

"The most powerful voice you will ever hear is the one you choose to believe."

We've traveled a long road together—one that began with identifying your inner critic and ends with something far more profound: the power to reclaim your own voice.

When I think back to that moment hanging off the cliff, I remember how quickly everything that once felt heavy, self-doubt, fear of judgment, the need for approval, just fell away. In that moment, only one question mattered: *Am I living the way I want to live? Am I leading the way I want to lead?*

This book wasn't written to give you more information; it was written to give you *permission*. Permission to step into your leadership with clarity, confidence, and courage.

Your story isn't defined by the voice of your inner critic. It's defined by the choices you make every single day.

Key Lessons to Remember:

- Your inner critic has a story. It was shaped by moments when shrinking felt safer than standing tall.
- The cost of listening is real. It shows up as burnout, hesitation, and a life that feels too small for your gifts.
- Naming and reframing are transformative. Disrupt old narratives by naming them, questioning their truth, and choosing a story that empowers you.

- Resilience is a practice. It grows every time you face discomfort and choose to show up with intention.
- Your voice matters. Especially when it shakes.

These aren't just ideas; they're strategies. But they only work if you put them into action.

Be Honest with Yourself:

- Where did you first hear the voice of your inner critic?
- What has it cost you to let that voice speak louder than your truth?
- What would be possible if you stopped waiting to be ready and decided to start now?

Your Final Challenge

In the next 30 days, take one small but powerful step:

1. Identify where your inner critic is still holding you back.

2. Choose one area of your leadership where you're ready to reclaim your voice.

3. Take one bold action—no matter how small—that honors your intention.

You don't have to figure this out alone.

An Invitation to Work Together

If you're ready to take your confidence, influence, and resilience to the next level, I'm here to help.

Through my proven coaching frameworks and workshops, I've helped leaders like you turn reflection into action, and action into results. Together, we'll cut through the noise, focus on what matters most, and create the momentum you need to lead with clarity and purpose.

Learn more and connect with me here:
https://michelledestefano.coach

Thank you for trusting me to guide you through this journey. The fact that you're here, doing this work, speaks volumes about your courage and commitment.

Your story isn't over. This is where it truly begins.

www.ingramcontent.com/pod-product-compliance
Lightning Source LLC
Chambersburg PA
CBHW040929210326
41597CB00030B/5234